Traverse REGION

Doing post card photography in this region for many years has given me a wonderful opportunity to explore the Grand Traverse region in depth. From busy downtown Traverse City to remote places on South Manitou Island where gulls nest; on land, from a boat or from the air, this truly is a remarkable part of America.

John Penrod

Michigan's highway M-22 is considered one of the state's most scenic routes. It follo
the shoreline of Lake Michigan from Manistee to Northport and back to Traverse City.
Traveling north along West Michigan's shoreline as one enters Benzie County, the
become larger and more spread out providing great vistas overlooking lakes, rivers
a few villages. To the west, Lake Michigan reaches to the horizon and beyond. In t
formative years of development, the lake became the prime means of transportation i
this area.

Winter at Frankfort is shown in a photo taken in the early 1960's as a car ferry i
entering the harbor. Now discontinued, the Ann Arbor Railroad operated the auto a

A

C

D

ilroad car ferry service year around between Elberta, Michigan and
rts in Wisconsin. The Frankfort harbor now is primarily a port for
hing and pleasure boating.

From the aerial view, one can appreciate the vast amount of water
rounding Frankfort. Crystal Lake and the face of the Sleeping Bear
nes can be seen in the distance. This is a favorite place for gliders
d hang gliding where a prevailing westerly wind pushes against the
gh bank at Elberta causing an updraft that can keep a glider airborne
r long periods of time.

Traverse
REGION

B

E

A: *Winter at Frankfort*
B: *U.S. Coast Guard Station*
C: *Frankfort North Breakwater Light*
D: *Crystal Lake*
E: *Scenic Overlook, M-22*
F: *Aerial View, Frankfort*

F

In this region there are so many lovely places with public access, it seems the best has been saved for everyone to enjoy. This is certainly true within the Sleeping Bear National Lakeshore. Just south of the village of Empire there is a small parking area where a foot trail leads to the Empire bluffs overlooking Lake Michigan. The scene from there is so inspirational that it is well worth the walk. Far below is Empire and the panorama view sweeps out over the lake and back towa

A: *Beulah*
B: *View From Empire Bluffs*
C: *Platte River at Lake Michigan*
D: *Canoeing on the Platte River*
E: *Robert H. Manning Memorial Lighthouse*

A

C

atte River Point to the south. The Platte River flows west
ssing into Platte Lake and then on to join Lake Michigan at
s point. Canoeing down the Platte River is a favorite family
ort. The water is crystal clear and the scenery delightful.
Michigan's newest lighthouse is located at the public beach at
pire. There is also a marker with a map that tells about the
derwater preserve in the Manitou Passage where many ships
ve been lost.

Traverse
R E G I O N

B

E

D

Sleeping Bear Dunes is a unique formation of sand that rises 450 feet above the Lake Michigan water level. The exposed sand facing the lake erodes as the sun and wind loosen the grains and layers, allowing the sand to slide down to the lake. In some areas layers of sand that were deposited thousands of years ago are being returned to the lake at the rate of a foot a year.

It is a remarkable region with outstanding scenery. On calm days, nearby lakes and ponds mirror the dune images.

A

C

end of the Sleeping Bear

ans tell of a mother bear and her two cubs who long ago tried to n across Lake Michigan. Nearing this shore, the exhausted cubs ed behind. Mother bear climbed to the top of a bluff to watch wait for her offspring. They never reached her and today she can be seen as the "Sleeping Bear," a solitary dune covered with trees and shrubs. Her hapless cubs are the Manitou Islands that short distance away.

B

A: *Aerial View of*
   Sleeping Bear Dunes
B: *Dunes at Dawn*
   from Empire Beach
C: *Dune Reflections*
D: *Sleeping Bear*
   Dunes with South
   Manitou Island

D

At one time dune rides operated out of Glen Haven on the north end of the dunes. When the dunes became a National Lakeshore, driving on the dunes was discontinued. Now, visit can drive through the park on Pierce Stocking Drive, a 7.4 mi trip with parking places at a dozen scenic points of interest. A number of wooden walks and elevated platforms allow visitor enjoy the dunes and still protect the fragile ecology.

A

B

A: Panorama
of the Dunes
B: Trees and
Grass on the
Dunes
C: Grass and
Sand Patterns
D: Viewing
Platforms

is said that Mother Nature does not like to see the earth
vered, and this is proven here at Sleeping Bear Dunes. In
ast fifty years, vegetation that is adaptable to the sand
covered much of the dunes. The trees and grass stabilize
dunes and sand movement. One area of the park that has
changed much is "The Climb." Here the sand is one huge
ground.

D

"The Climb" is a huge sand drift, hundreds of feet high, th will challenge anyone's climbing skill. From a distance, it loc deceptively easy. It is not! The sand is soft, smooth and feels good and if you fall you will have a soft landing. Looking ov your shoulder the parking lot gets smaller with each step, and higher you climb the larger Glen Lake looks. Once at the top reward is a wonderful view of both Lake Michigan and Glen Lake. Now, the fun part is the giant steps needed while runnir back down the dune.

A:

A: "The Climb", a Sand
Mountain
B: "The Climb"
C: Fun in the Sand
D: View Toward Glen Lake
E: South Manitou Island
Lighthouse
F: Sleeping Bear Coast Guard
Station
G: Herring Gull Chick
H: Francisco Morizon

B

C

D

The South Manitou Island Lighthouse was built in 1871 to [gui]de ships through the Manitou Passage. The Sleeping Bear [Co]ast Guard Station started in 1909, at Glen Haven, as a part of [the] United States Life Saving Service. It operated until 1944. Having run aground, the rusting hull of the freighter Francisco [M]orizon is near South Manitou Island. Barn swallows swoop [thr]ough the portholes to nest inside. Herring gulls also find this a [saf]e place to make nests.

E

F

G

H

12

Aerial View of Leland and Lake Leelanau

elanau County's picturesque village of Leland is a
pular resort community along the shore of Lake
chigan. It is a unique fishtown, vacation area and
eway to North and South Manitou Islands. Enjoy lunch
ng the waterfront, visit the fish market for fresh or
oked fish, stroll around town and go shopping in the
ny interesting stores and gift shops.

A

B

C

D

A: Dining Along the
    Waterfront
B: Fish Nets
C: Picturesque Harbor
D: Sunset Over Lake
    Michigan

The Leelanau Peninsula reaches northward into Lake Michig
forming Grand Traverse Bay. If lower Michigan is in the shape
a mitten, then the peninsula is the little finger.

Near the tip is the town of Northport with a picturesque
sheltered harbor on Grand Traverse Bay. Further north at the tip
of the point is Leelanau State Park and Grand Traverse
Lighthouse. The lighthouse is completely restored and is a
museum open to the public. Visitors have the opportunity to str

A

A: Leelanau State Park
B: Northport Marina
C: Grand Traverse
    Lighthouse
D: Fresnel Lens
    Display
E: Beach Stone
    Birdhouse
F: Northport
G: Restored Bedroom
H: Living Room
    Heating Stove

B

F

grounds and tour the inside where the lighthouse keepers
[li]ved. There is a wealth of historical information, photographs,
[furn]iture and artifacts on display. Some of the keepers' beach
[sto]ne artistry is still in use as stair steps, flower planters and even
[a] one birdhouse.

On the bay side of the peninsula near Omena is the Native
[Am]erican community of Pshawbestown. It is frequently the site
[of a] colorful Pow Wow.

D

C

E

G

H

Grand Traverse Lighthouse

Lakes and waterways abound in the Traverse Region and the highways are scenic. Highway M-22 winds along the Grand Traverse Bay through Suttons Bay and on to Traverse City.

Lake Leelanau, in this area, is a very long lake consisting of two parts. The town of Lake Leelanau is at the narrows that connect the two bodies of water.

A

C

D

E

During the summer months Interlochen National Music Camp draws [tale]nted students from around the world. They combine their musical skills [to] provide visitors an opportunity to enjoy a great variety of concerts. [Wal]king through the camp, music seems to come from everywhere as the [sou]nd of students at practice drifts through the trees. At the final [per]formance of the season, over a thousand campers perform Liszt's Les [Prel]udes before a huge audience.

Traverse
REGION

B

A: Lake Ann,
   Headwaters of the
   Platte River
B: Village of Lake
   Leelanau
C: Interlochen
   National Music
   Camp
D: Les Preludes at
   Interlochen
E: Suttons Bay
F: Big Wheels from
   the Lumbering Era
   at Interlochen
   State Park

F

The geographic location at the foot of Grand Traverse Bay, where the natural land travel routes crisscrossed, made this reg an ideal place for a settlement. Surrounded by the pristine beau of the bays, rivers and lakes, Traverse City has grown to be the largest city in the northern part of Michigan. There are hotels a accommodations of all kinds. Restaurants, malls and shopping opportunities of great variety are sure to please everyone. In sp of the growth, downtown and the tree-lined Front Street still retains its charm.

A

A: Traverse City
B: Boardman River
C: Swimming Beach at Clinch Park
D: Front Street
E: City Opera House Built 1891
F: Autumn Decoration on Front Street
G: Miniature Steam Train, Clinch Park

D

E

H

Summer brings more visitors, but there is outdoor activity all r around. Autumn adds lots of beautiful fall color to the dwood forests. In winter downhill and cross country skiing are ular sports as well as snowmobile events and dog sledding. ingtime has wild flowers and some of the best morel shroom hunting in the state. Since Traverse City is the "Cherry ital of the World," the surrounding orchards become white n blossoms in the month of May.

B

C

F

G

J

H: Christmas Lights on Front Street
I: Duncan L. Clinch Yacht Harbor
J: Tall Ship Excursions on Traverse Bay

Michigan is the world's largest producer of tart cherries a[nd] Traverse City has the honor of being the "Cherry Capital of [the] World." Here the temperature is moderate and stabilized by L[ake] Michigan. In springtime the cool water helps to keep the tree[s] from budding too early reducing the danger from frost. The s[oil in] this region is ideal for fruit trees.

When the tart cherries ripen, the fruit is harvested with a [

A

B

D

aker. The shaker looks like a large inverted umbrella that wraps around e tree. Then, an arm reaches in to the trunk and gives it a quick shake. herries roll down the canvas to the center where a conveyor lifts them to waiting tanks of cold water. The cherries are transported to the pro-essing plants in tanks of water, thus avoiding any damage to the elicate fruit.

Wonderful taste-tempting sweet and tart cherries products are offered roughout the region by farm markets.

C

F

A: Tart Cherries
B: Sweet Cherries
C: Orchard Scene Near
    Suttons Bay
D: Cherry Festival,
    Traverse City
E: Blossom Time
F: Cherry Shaker

E

The Old Mission Peninsula is a long arm of land that extends
northward from Traverse City dividing Grand Traverse Bay into
two parts. The scenery here is outstanding. Beautiful orchards and
vineyards spread across the rolling hills in stark contrast with the
deep blue water beyond.

Because of the climate, the peninsula has ideal growing
conditions for wine grapes and there are several excellent

A

B

C

H

I

...eries here. Old Mission Point Lighthouse and the historic ...ssler log home are located at the tip of the peninsula. This spot ...alfway between the Equator and the North Pole on the 45th ...allel.

...The Cherry Center Grange No. 1850 has erected a memorial in ...or of the men and women of Peninsula Town who served in ...rld Wars I and II.

Traverse
REGION

D

E

F

G

A: Vineyard Scene
B: Hybrid Wine Grapes
C: Ida Red Apples
D: Old Mission Point
    Lighthouse
E: 45th Parallel Marker
F: Hessler Log Home
G: Old Mission
H: Fine Wines
I: Sunset Over the Bay
J: Haserot Beach

J

The Music House, located just north of Acme, is a fascinating museum music making machines. Its concept is to preserve many of the priceless original creations and to share their heritage with as many interested people as possible. They also restore and preserve many historic items of local interest. The Music House features a large collection of automated musical instruments with live performances from displays in village settings.

The "Acme General Store" is a turn-of-the-century setting for the 1899 Regina Corona music box that plays 27-inch discs. The "Hurry Back Saloon" one of Traverse City's turn-of-the-century finest, is a setting for Losch and

A

B

C

Nickelodeons. They are part of a large collection of rare automatic
...ue musical instruments which are the theme of The Music House.
...ed tours acquaint guests with the sound of yesterday and the
...cate and clever, often beautiful machines which produced it.
...olfing is one of the most popular activities in the Traverse region.
...d Traverse Resort, just northeast of Traverse City is the area's
...st resort and golf center. Dominating the entire landscape is the 15
... tower which features luxury rooms, suites and a
...nificent restaurant on the top floor.

D

E

F

G

A: *Acme General Store*
B: *The Mortier*
C: *Hurry Back Saloon*
D: *Aerial of Grand*
 Traverse Resort
E: *Golfing Enthusiasts*
F: *Grand Traverse Resort*
G: *Colorful Landmark*

To the north and east of Traverse City is a cluster of inland lakes that provide lovely shorelines for homes and cottages as well as all of the associated water sports. The water in these la[kes] is very clear and when viewed from the air one can see an interesting variety of color changes along the edges due to the

A

C

A: Kewadin, Elk Lake
B: Torch River
C: Alden Waterfront
D: Alden Depot Park &
Museum
E: Sailing on Torch Lake
F: Eastport, Torch Lake

D

of the water. Most of this lake region is in Antrim County.
o borders Grand Traverse Bay and Lake Michigan.
the upper tip of Elk Lake is the village of Kewadin. The
nunity of Alden is located on the east side of Torch Lake.

B

E

F

Elk Lake joins the waters of Grand Traverse Bay and Lak[e]
Michigan at Elk Rapids. A dam controls the water level on E[lk]
Lake and the water passes through a hydroelectric plant.

Elk Rapids is a beautiful community and the residents tak[e]
great pride in their gardens and floral plantings. The Edward[s]
Grace Memorial Harbor has one of the best marinas and boa[t]
launching facilities in the region.

A

B

C

Further north in Antrim County is Central Lake, a long narrow [lak]e providing excellent boating and fishing opportunities. [K]alkaska has many rivers and streams and a large portion of [Kal]kaska County is state forest and public land. It is well known [for] its great trout fishing. Each year a trout festival is held to [cele]brate the opening of the season.

Traverse

REGION

D

E

G

F

A: *Elk Rapids*
B: *Central Lake*
C: *Trout Fountain,*
   Kalkaska
D: *Sailboats at Elk Rapids*
E: *Fishing Below the*
   Hydro Plant
F: *Footbridge to Island*
   House, Elk Rapids
G: *Edward C. Grace*
   Memorial Harbor

There is something almost magical about this part of Michigan. For those who live here, it is a nice place to come home to and for those who do not, it is a wonderful place to visit. There is a certain atmosphere present that seems to give everyone a greater zest for living. One cannot be sure if the hills are bigger or just seem to be. The scenic vistas certainly are awesome. Anyone who has traveled on Highway M-37 on the Old Mission Peninsula and stopped to look at the view, probably found themselves slowly turning in a circle trying to scope out the 360 degree panorama. There are many special and unique natural places as well as fine stores, restaurants and accommodations so everyone who visits will want to return.